OPERATION BACKHANDER

1944 BATTLE FOR CAPE GLOUCESTER

DANIEL WRINN

CONTENTS

GET YOUR FREE COPY OF WW2: SPIES, SNIPERS AND THE WORLD AT WAR

Never miss a new release by signing up for my free readers group. Learn of special offers and interesting details I find in my research. You'll also get WW2: Spies, Snipers and Tales of the World at War delivered to your inbox. (You can unsubscribe at any time.) Go to danielwrinn.com to sign up

Behind our gun position we dug a depression that a couple of guys could lay in. That depression would fill with water, and at nighttime, when you wanted to take a nap, two guys would crawl in that water and their bodies would keep it warm. There was a drawback to that because your skin would all shrink up.

— SAM NICHOLAS, 1ST DIVISION MARINES

INTRODUCTION

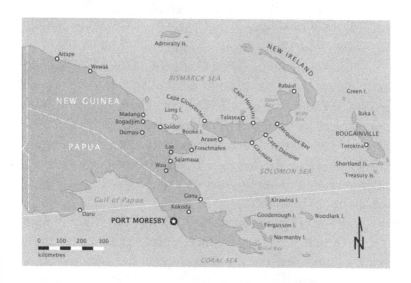

Early on the morning of December 26, 1943, Marines stood ready off the coast of Japanese-dominated New Britain. The outline of the mile-high Mount Talawe was just visible in the twilight. American and Australian cruisers shattered the early morning calm with ammunition flying from their destroyers' guns. The 1st Marine Division, was commanded by Major General William H. Rupertus, arriving from the recently finished Guadalcanal Campaign. The men steeled their nerves, waiting for daylight and the signal to assault the Yellow Beaches near Cape Gloucester.

Fire support ships blazed away for ninety minutes. They attempted to neutralize entire areas rather than destroy pinpointed targets because the dense jungle concealed most of the individual Japanese fortifications and ammunition dumps.

At dawn on D-Day, Army airmen joined the bombardment. B-24 Liberator bombers flew at such an altitude that the Marines could barely see them. They dropped five-hundred-pound bombs on the beaches, scoring a hit on one of the enemy fuel dumps at the Cape Gloucester airfield—releasing a fiery geyser that leapt hundreds of feet into the air. A squadron of B-25 medium bombers and A-20 light bombers followed them, attacking from a lower altitude, hammering the Japanese antiaircraft batteries.

Then the attention shifted to the assault beaches. Landing craft carrying two battalions of the 7th Marines started toward the shore. An LCI (Landing Craft, Infantry), with multiple rocket launchers, took positions on the flank of the first wave bound for each beach. They unleashed a hellish barrage, keeping the Japanese troops pinned down after the destroyers and cruisers shifted their fire to avoid putting the assault troops in danger.

At 0745, Higgins boats brought the first wave toward Yellow Beach 1. They grounded onto a narrow strip of volcanic sand that measured just under five hundred yards from one end to the other, bringing the 3rd Battalion Marines' lead elements. Two minutes later, the 1st Battalion landed on Yellow Beach 2. Separated by a thousand yards of jungle and a seven-hundred-yard shoreline. Neither battalion encountered any organized resistance. The Marines used a smoke-screen that drifted across the beaches. This hampered the later waves of landing craft and blinded Japanese observers on Target Hill overlooking the beachhead. No enemy manned the log-and-earth bunkers that might have raked the assault force with deadly fire.

The Yellow Beaches on the north coast of the peninsula pointed west toward Cape Gloucester. Codenamed Operation Backhander, this access point was the primary objective: two airfields at the cape's northwestern tip. By capturing the airfields, the 1st Marine Division would allow Allied airmen to step up attacks on the Japanese fortress at Rabaul, three hundred miles away at the northeastern edge of New Britain —the opposite end of the long, crescent-shaped island. The capture of these Yellow Beaches was vital for the New Britain Campaign, but two additional landings also took place. The first occurred on December 15, landing at Cape Merkus on Arawe Bay along the south coast. The second at Green Beach on the northwest coast, also on December 26.

The Cape Merkus landing was across the channel from the islet of Arawe. Its purposes were to disrupt motorized barges and other Japanese small-craft moving men and supplies along the southern coast of New Britain and to divert attention from Cape Gloucester. The Marine amphibian tractor crews used the slower and more vulnerable LVT-1 Alligators and the new armored LVT-2 Water Buffaloes to carry soldiers from the 112th Cavalry to make landings on Orange Beach at the western edge of Cape Merkus.

The destroyer *Conyngham* provided fire support enhanced by rocket equipped DUKW's (a 2.5-ton, six-wheel, am-phibious truck known as duck) and a submarine chaser desig-nated as the control craft. A last-minute bombing silenced the beach defenses and enabled the LVT Water Buffaloes to crush enemy machine guns that survived the opening bombardment.

Two diversionary landings by soldiers paddling ashore in rubber boats were less successful. Savage enemy fire forced one group to turn back just short of its objective on Orange

Beach, but the other gained a foothold on Pilelo Island and killed the small group of Japanese defenders. Enemy airmen reported the assault force approaching Cape Merkus. Japanese bombers and fighters from Rabaul attacked within two hours of the landing. The Japanese executed sporadic airstrikes throughout December with diminishing ferocity. They ultimately shifted their troops to meet the threat in the south.

Then there was the secondary landing on December 26. Battalion Landing Team 21 was a 1,500 man assault force, from the 2/1 Marines, commanded by Lieutenant Colonel James Masters. They started toward Green Beach supported by American destroyers *Smith* and *Reid* with their 5-inch naval gunfire. LCMs (Landing Craft, Medium) carried amphibian trucks, driven by soldiers, fitted with rocket launchers. They fired from the landing craft as the assault force attacked the beach. The first wave landed at 0750, with two others closely following ashore. The Marines carved out a beachhead 1,200 yards wide and 500 yards inland, encountering no opposition. Their mission was to sever the coastal trail that passed west of Mount Talawe and prevent Japanese from reinforcements reaching the Cape Gloucester airfields.

Following the coastal trail proved more difficult than expected. The local villagers tilled and cleared garden plots, leaving them for the jungle to reclaim. This left a maze of trails—some fresh, some faint—but most led nowhere. The Japanese did not take advantage of the confusion caused by the path tangling until early morning on December 30. They attacked the Green Beach force and took advantage of the heavy rain that muffled sounds and reduced visibility. When the Japanese began their assault, the Marines called down mortar fire within 20 yards of their defensive positions. A battery of the 11th Marines was reorganized as an infantry unit because the cannoneers couldn't find suitable targets for their 75mm howitzers.

Gunnery Sergeant Guiseppe Guilano materialized at critical moments and fired a light machine gun from his hip. His bravery and cool disdain for danger earned him a Navy Cross. While some Japanese troops penetrated the position, a counterattack led by Company G drove them off. This brutal fighting cost the Marines six dead and seventeen wounded. Ninety Japanese soldiers perished, and five surrendered.

ESTABLISHING THE BEACHHEAD

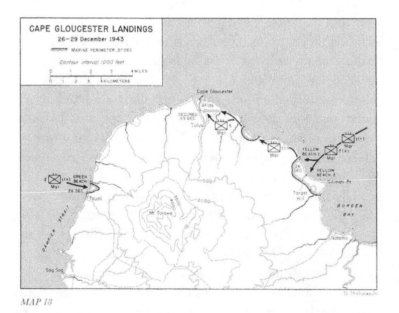

CAPE GLOUCESTER LANDINGS
26–29 December 1943

MARINE PERIMETER, 27 DEC

Contour interval 1000 feet

MAP 18

THE JAPANESE HAD a mixture of combat and service troops in western New Britain. They used motorized barges to shuttle cargo and troops along the coast from Rabaul to Cape

Gloucester. They utilized their fleet of trawlers and schooners enhanced by destroyers from the Japanese Navy for any more extended movements.

Japanese troops that defended western New Britain were known as the *Matsuda Force*. General Iwao Matsuda was a military transportation specialist and a commander of an infantry regiment in Manchuria. When he arrived in February 1943 on New Britain, he took control of the battle-tested *141st Infantry* from the Philippines conquest and additional antiaircraft and artillery units. Matsuda established his headquarters near Kalingi, the coastal trail northwest of Mount Talawe, five miles from the airfields at Cape Gloucester. He ultimately changed his location to reflect his tactical challenges.

The Allies increased their threat to New Britain as 1943 wore on. Japanese headquarters at Rabaul assigned Gen. Matsuda's force to the *17th Division* under Lieutenant General Sakai, recently arriving from Shanghai. Sakai's division was attacked en route and lost two of their four transports to submarine torpedoes and mines. An Allied air attack nearly wiped out the third convoy. This deprived the Japanese defenders of three thousand replacement and service troops. LtGen. Sakai deployed the remainder of his forces to western New Britain under Matsuda's tactical command.

The mid-December Cape Merkus landings caused Gen. Matsuda to shift his troops to combat the threat. This redeployment did not account for the lack of resistance at the Yellow Beaches. Matsuda was familiar with the terrain of western New Britain. He did not believe the Americans would storm the small strips of sand that extended a few yards inland, backing up to a swamp. Matsuda did not know the American maps labeled the beaches as a "swamp forest." Even though the aerial photography taken after the initial preliminary airstrikes revealed no shadow within the bomb craters—there was evidence of a water level high enough to fill these depressions to the brim. Matsuda knew the airfields were the obvious prize and did not believe that the Marines would plunge into the muck and risk becoming bogged down short of achieving their objective.

Matsuda forfeited the immediate advantage of opposing the Marine assault force at the water's edge. Enemy troops were suffering the long-term indirect effects of eroding Japanese fortunes, beginning at Guadalcanal and New Guinea. The Allies dominated the skies over New Britain, blunted any air attacks on the beach at Cape Merkus beach-head, and bombed at will throughout the island. While the airstrikes did minor damage, except for Rabaul, they demoralized the Japanese troops suffering from medicine and supply shortages because of the submarine and air attacks. An ineffective network of primitive trails hugged the coastline and increased Gen. Matsuda's dependence on barges. The capture of Cape Merkus made his barges, convoys, and coastal shipping vulnerable to aircraft, and later to gunboats and torpedo craft.

The two battalions that landed on the Yellow Beaches crossed the sands and plunged through a wall of undergrowth into a swamp forest. A Marine could slog through knee-deep mud, step into a hole, and then end up damp to his neck. A Japanese counterattack while the Marines lurched through the swamp forest could have inflicted severe casualties. Gen. Matsuda lacked the roads and vehicles to shift his troops in time to take advantage of the terrain. The Japanese defenders were immobile on the ground and tried to retaliate by air. A flight of enemy aircraft sent from Rabaul was intercepted by Army P-38s. Two Japanese bombers evaded the Army fighter planes and sank the destroyer *Brownson* with a direct hit, followed by an immense explosion. She took 108 crewmen with her; the rest were rescued by destroyers *Daly* and *Lamson*.

When the first Japanese bombers came into view, a

squadron of Army B-25s flew over LSTs (Landing Ships, Tank) attacking targets at Borgen Bay, south of the Yellow Beaches. Gunners on board the LSTs opened fire at the enemy aircraft but mistook friend for foe and shot down two American bombers and damaged two others. The Allied planes, shaken by the experience, dropped their bombs too soon on the 11th Marines' artillery positions at the left flank of Yellow Beach 1—killing one Marine and wounding fifteen others. A Marine battalion commander from the artillery regiment later wrote:

It was like trying to dig a hole with my nose as the bombs exploded. Trying to get down into the ground just a little bit more.

By the afternoon of D-Day, the 1st Marine Division had established a beachhead. The 7th Marines' assault battalions had pushed ahead and captured Target Hill on the left flank before pausing to await reinforcements. Two more battalions arrived during the day: Landing Team 31 came ashore at 0815 on Yellow Beach 1. They weaved through the 3/7 Marines and veered to the northwest, leading the way toward the airfields at 0845. The 2/7 Marines landed and waded through the swamp forest between the 1st and 3rd Battalions, expanding the beachhead. The next infantry unit was the 1/1 Marines, reaching Yellow Beach 1 at 1300 to join the 3rd Battalion advancing on the airfields. The 11th Marines, despite the accidental bombing, set up their artillery with the help of amphibian tractors. Some of the amphibious tractors brought the 75mm howitzers from the LSTs directly to the battery firing positions. Other tractors were used to break a trail through the undergrowth to pull the more massive 105mm weapons.

Army trucks loaded with supplies came ashore from the LSTs. Logistical plans called for these vehicles to move forward as mobile supply dumps, but the swamp forest proved impossible for the wheeled vehicles. Drivers abandoned their trucks to avoid being left behind when the ships moved out from the threat of Japanese bombers. The Marines built roads and corduroyed them with logs or shifted the cargo onto the amphibian tractors. Even with this enormous effort, the convoy still got underway with over 100 tons of supplies left on board.

While the cargo and reinforcements crossed the beach, the Marines advanced inland and encountered the first real Japanese resistance. On December 26 at 1015, the 3/1 Marines pushed ahead, forced into a column of companies by a swamp on the left flank that narrowed the frontage.

The Japanese opened fire from camouflaged bunkers, killing the commander of Company K and his executive officer. These sturdy Japanese bunkers proved impervious to the bazooka rockets, which failed to detonate in the soft earth covering the structures. And the 37mm guns could not penetrate the logs protecting the Japanese defenders.

An LVT-1 Alligator that had delivered supplies for Company K attempted to crush one bunker—but got wedged between two trees. Japanese snipers killed the tractor's two machine gunners before the driver could break it free. When the tractor lunged ahead, it caved in one bunker, silencing enemy fire and enabling Marines to isolate the three others and destroy them—killing twenty-five Japanese. A platoon of M4 Sherman tanks joined in to lead the advance beyond this first strongpoint.

Japanese troops of the *1st Debarkation Unit* provided the initial opposition, but Gen. Matsuda had alerted his nearby infantry units to converge onto the beachhead. A Japanese battalion moved into position late in the afternoon on D-Day. They were opposite the 2/7 Marines who clung to a crescent-shaped position with both flanks protected by marshlands.

After sunset, only muzzle flashes pierced the darkness as the firing intensity increased. The Japanese were preparing to counterattack. Amphibian tractors could not make supply runs until it was light enough to avoid the fallen tree trunks and roots when navigating through the swamp forest. Before dawn, Lieutenant Colonel "Chesty" Puller, the XO of the 7th Marines, organized the men of the service company and regimental headquarters into carrying parties. He loaded them with ammunition and waded with them through the dangerous swamp. Only one misstep and a Marine carrying bandoliers of rifle ammo or containers of mortar shells could slip, stumble, and drown.

When the regimental commander reinforced the Marines with Battery D, of the 1st Special Weapons Battalion, LtCol. Puller had the men leave the 37mm guns behind and carry the ammunition instead. A guide from headquarters met the column that LtCol. Puller had pressed into service. He led the Marines forward through a blinding downpour, driven sideways by a monsoon gale. Obscured landmarks forced the heavily laden Marines to blindly wade onward. Each man clung to the belt of the man in front. Not until 0805, over twelve hours after the column started its march, did the Marines reach their goal, put down their loads, and take up their rifles to fight.

The 2/7 Marines had been fighting for their lives since the first storm struck. A curtain of rain prevented mortar crews from seeing their aiming stakes. The battalion commander described these men firing as just "guessing by God's will." Mud got into most of the small arms ammo and jammed machine guns and rifles. Marines abandoned their water-filled foxholes while the defenders hung on fighting.

At dawn, Japanese soldiers moved toward the right flank of the 2/7 Marines, attempting to outflank them. They were possibly forced into that direction by the Marines' defensive fire. When Battery D arrived and moved into the threatened area, they forced the Japanese to break off their action and regroup.

DEFENSE OF HELL'S POINT

THE OVERALL PLAN for the 1st Division Marines' maneuver called for Combat Team C to take and hold a beachhead at Target Hill. Combat Team B would advance on the airfields. Due to the enemy build-up to prepare for the attack, Gen. Rupertus requested the release of the division reserve, Combat Team A, to reinforce the Marines. The Army agreed and sent the 1st, 2nd, and 3rd Battalions in support.

The division commander landed them on Blue Beach, three miles right of the Yellow Beaches. By using Blue Beach, this placed the 5th Marines closer to Cape Gloucester and the airfields. Not every element of Combat Team A received these orders. Several units touched down on the Yellow Beaches instead and moved on foot to their planned destination.

While Gen. Rupertus laid out plans to commit the reserve troops, Combat Team B advanced toward the airfields. Marines initially encountered light resistance but were warned of a maze of trenches and bunkers stretching inland from a promontory—earning the name Hell's Point. Japanese troops built these defenses to protect the beaches where Gen. Matsuda had expected the Allies to land. The 3/1 Marines attacked the Hell's Point position on the flank instead of a head-on frontal assault. Overrunning this complex set of defenses proved a lethal task.

Rupertus delayed the attack to give the division reserve, the 5th Marines, time to come ashore. On December 28, after the 2/11 Marines and Army A-20s bombarded the dug-in enemy, the assault troops suffered another delay. They waited several hours for a platoon of M4 Sherman medium tanks to increase the attack's intensity. At 1100, the 3/1 Marines moved ahead. Company I and the medium Sherman's led the way. At the same time, Company A waded through jungle and swamp intending to seize the ridge's inland point extending from Hell's Point. Despite the obstacles in their path, Company A surged from the jungle at 1145, crossing the tall grass field until repulsed by intense enemy fire. By late afternoon, Company A broke off the attack. Attackers and defenders were short of ammunition and exhausted. The 2/11 Marines covered Company A's withdrawal behind an onslaught of fire. By nightfall, the Japanese had abandoned their positions.

The attached Shermans with Company I collided head-on with the primary defenses fifteen minutes after Company A assaulted inland of the ridge. The Japanese had modified their defenses since the December 26 landings. They hacked fire lanes in the undergrowth, cut new gun ports and bunkers, and moved men and weapons to oppose the Allied attack along the coastal trail parallel to the shore instead of over the beach. The Marines advanced in drenching rain and encountered jungle-covered enemy positions protected by mines and barbed wire.

Medium Sherman tanks, protected by riflemen, crushed the bunkers and weapons inside. Company I drifted to the left flank during the fight, and Company K, reinforced with a platoon of Sherman tanks, closed the gap between the coastal track and Hell's Point. This unit used the same tactics as Company I. A rifle squad followed each of the Shermans after the tanks cracked the twelve bunkers and fired inside. The riflemen killed anyone attempting to fight or flee. Nine Marines were killed and thirty-six were wounded in this assault while over two hundred and sixty Japanese died fighting.

After the Marines shattered the Hell's Point defenses, two battalions of the 5th Marines joined in the airfield's advance. The 1st and 2nd Battalions moved out in a column. In front of the Marines was a swamp only a few inches deep. The downpour increased the depth to over five feet making it hard for the shorter Marines. The 5th Marines lost time wading through the swamp. This delayed the attack while the leading elements chose a piece of open and dry ground to establish a perimeter while the remaining Marines caught up.

The 1/1 Marines encountered only scattered resistance— mostly sniper fire—as they weaved along the coast beyond Hell's Point. Advancing with half-tracks carrying 75mm guns, artillery, medium Sherman's, and even rocket-firing DUKWs, the 1st Marines held a line extended inland from the coast. The 3/1 Marines and the 2/5 Marines advanced on the flanks and formed a semicircle around the airfield.

Colonel Sumiya of the *53rd Infantry Regiment* was the Japanese officer in charge of defending the airfields. On December 29, he fell back to gain time. Sumiya gathered the surviving troops for Razorback Hill's defense, a ridge running diagonally across the southwestern approaches to the airfield. The 5th Marines attacked on December 30, supported by artillery and tanks. Sumiya's troops had built sturdy bunkers, but the chest-high grass covering Razorback Hill did not stop the Allied assault like the jungle at Hell's Point. The Imperial Japanese fought bravely to hold their position, even stalling the Marines' advance. But the Japanese had neither the firepower nor the numbers to overcome. During the Japanese assault, one platoon of Company F beat back three *banzai* attacks.

Medium Shermans allowed the Marines to smash the remaining bunkers in their path and kill the enemy troops within. By nightfall on December 30, the Marine landing force overran the airfield defenses. At noon the next day, Gen. Rupertus hoisted the American flag next to the wreckage of a Japanese bomber at Airfield No. 2—the larger of the airstrips.

The 1st Marine Division seized the objective for the Battle of Cape Gloucester. But the airstrips proved only marginal value to the Allies. Airfield No. 1 was overgrown with sharp, tall kunai grass. Craters from American bombs pockmarked the surface of Airfield No. 2. After its capture, Japanese hit-and-run planes added more bomb craters, despite antiaircraft fire from the 12th Defense Battalion. Army aviation engineers worked desperately around the clock to get Airfield No. 2 back in operation. This task took until the end of January 1944.

Army aircraft based here defended against air assaults for as long as Rabaul remained an active Japanese airbase.

CROSSING SUICIDE CREEK

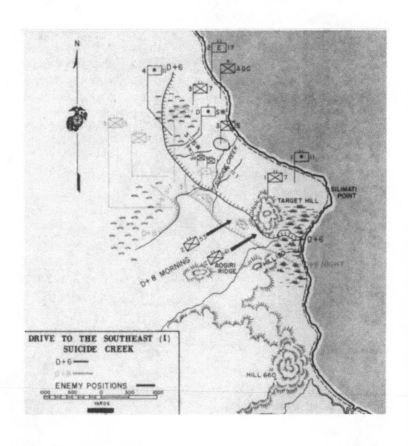

DRIVE TO THE SOUTHEAST (I)
SUICIDE CREEK

D+6
ENEMY POSITIONS

WHILE MAJOR GENERAL Rupertus directed the airfields' capture, Brigadier General Lemuel Shepherd had come ashore on December 26 and took command of the beachhead. Shepherd had coordinated the logistics activity and assumed responsibility to expand the perimeter southwest and secure Borgen Bay's shores. He used a shore party of engineers, transportation, and service troops to handle the logistics. The 3/5 Marines arrived on December 30 to help the 7th Marines enlarge the beachhead.

Gen. Shepherd had limited knowledge of the Japanese deployments to the south and west of the Yellow Beaches. Thick vegetation concealed swamps, streams, ridgelines, trenches, and bunkers. The progress made toward the airfields showed a Japanese weakness in that area and a potential strength in Borgen Bay and the Yellow Beaches vicinity. To resolve the uncertainty of the enemy's intentions and numbers, Gen. Shepherd issued orders to probe enemy defenses on January 1, 1944.

Colonel Katayama commanded the *141st Infantry* and prepared a counterattack. Katayama intended to hurl three reinforced battalions against the Allies at Target Hill. Japanese headquarters believed 2,500 Marines were now ashore on New Britain, 10% of the total. Col. Katayama thought his force was strong enough to do this job.

Katayama waited and gathered his strength, giving Gen. Shepherd time to make the first move. Midmorning on January 2, the 1/7 Marines stood ready near Target Hill. The 2nd Battalion waited along a stream known as Suicide Creek. The 3/5 Marines advanced into the jungle to cover the 3/7 Marines on one flank. As the units pivoted, they would cross Suicide Creek to squeeze out of the 2/7th Marines and provide Shepherd with a reserve.

The change in direction through thick vegetation proved exceptionally difficult. In the words of one Marine:

You'd step from your line, take ten paces, and turn around to guide your buddy, and nobody was there. I can tell you it was a very small war and a very lonely business.

The Japanese troops were dug in south of Suicide Creek. From there, they resisted every attempt by the Marines to cross the stream that day. This created a stalemate until Seabees from Company C built a corduroy road. They punched through the swamp forest behind the Yellow Beaches for the tanks to move forward and smash through enemy defenses.

While Marines waited at Suicide Creek on Sherman tanks, Katayama attacked Target Hill. He took advantage of the darkness. His infantry cut steps into the lower slopes so troops could climb more efficiently. The Japanese followed their preconceived plan, to the letter, of advancing up the steps and slipping past the Company A, 7th Marines' thinly held lines. At midnight enemy troops stormed the strongest of the company's defenses. Japanese mortars fired to soften the defenses and screen the approach. Still, they could not conceal the sound of the soldiers working their way up the hill, and the Marines were ready. While Japanese supporting fire proved to be inaccurate, one round did score a direct hit on a machine gun position killing the gunner and wounding two others. The injured Marines kept on firing their weapon until someone else could take over. This lone gun fired over five thousand rounds and helped stop the Japanese thrust, ending at dawn. The Japanese could not crack the 1/7 Marines' lines or loosen their grip on Target Hill.

. . .

A dead Japanese officer on Target Hill had documents that cast a new light on enemy defenses south of Suicide Creek. On a crudely drawn map, Aogiri Ridge was discovered. This enemy strongpoint was unknown to Gen. Shepherd's intelligence section. Observers on Target Hill searched for the Aogiri Ridge trail network, but the jungle canopy frustrated their efforts.

Marine patrols on Target Hill found dozens of enemy bodies. They captured documents that, when translated, listed forty-seven killed Japanese and fifty-five wounded. Using field glasses to scan the jungle south of Suicide Creek, the 17th Marines finished the road to allow the Sherman tanks to test the stream's defenses.

On the afternoon of January 3, three Sherman tanks reached the creek. They realized the bank dropped off too sharply for them to negotiate. The engineers called in a bulldozer; they lowered its blade to gouge out the lip of the embankment. The Japanese realized the danger if the tanks could cross the creek and opened fire on the bulldozer, wounding the driver. A Marine climbed into the exposed driver seat until he was also wounded. Another Marine jumped forward, but instead of climbing onto the machine, he walked alongside and used its bulk for cover. He manipulated the controls with an ax handle and a shovel. By dark, he'd finished the job of converting the impossible bank into a ramp the Shermans could cross.

At dawn on January 4, the first Sherman went down the ramp and across the stream. As the tank emerged on the other side, Marines cut down two Japanese soldiers trying to detonate mines against the tank's sides. Other Shermans followed, accompanied by infantry, and smashed open the bunkers barring the way. The 3/7 Marines surged across the creek and joined the other battalions on the far right of the line that crossed the jungle, concealing Japanese defenses at Aogiri Ridge.

Now across Suicide Creek, the Marines advanced on Aogiri Ridge, another name for Hill 150. The Marine advance rapidly took the hill, but the Japanese resistance in the vicinity did not stop. Enemy fire wounded the commanding officer of the 3/5 Marines and killed his executive officer. On the morning of January 8, Lieutenant Colonel Lewis W. Walt, the executive officer of the 5th Marines, took command of the 3rd Battalion. Walt continued the attack from the previous day. His Marines encountered savage fire, and through the thick jungle they moved up a steep slope. The battalion formed a perimeter and dug in as night approached. Sudden skirmishes and random Japanese fire punctuated the darkness. The determined resistance and nature of the terrain convinced LtCol. Walt that he had a fight on his hands for Aogiri Ridge.

Drenching rain, mud, and rampaging streams blunted the shock action and firepower of the tanks. The heaviest weapon the Marines could bring forward was a 37mm gun. The 11th Marines hammered the crest of Aogiri Ridge while the 7th Marines probed the flanks. The 3/5 Marines advanced in the center, seizing a narrow segment of the slope. By nightfall, LtCol. Walt reported that his men had "reached the limit of their physical endurance and morale was low. It was now a question of whether they could hold their hard-earned gains."

The Marine crew of the 37mm gun opened fire to support the afternoon's last attack. After only two rounds, four of the nine men handling the weapon were wounded. LtCol. Walt called for volunteers. When no one responded, he crawled to the gun and pushed the weapon up the incline. After firing two more rounds and cutting a swath to the undergrowth, his third-round destroyed an enemy machine gun. From there, other Marines took over, and the new volunteers cut down the enemy. The new 37mm improvised gun crew continued to fire canister rounds every few yards until they manhandled the weapon to the crest. From there, the Marines dug in 10 yards away from bunkers the Japanese had built on the crest of the reverse slope.

At 0130 on January 10, the Japanese charged through a curtain of rain, firing and shouting as they attacked. The Marines clinging to the ridge repelled this attack and the three others that followed, costing the Marines nearly all of their ammunition. Marine reinforcements scaled the muddy slope with clips and belts of ammo for the machine guns and rifles. Still, there was hardly any time to distribute the ammunition before the Japanese launched their fifth attack of the morning. Marine artillery decimated the enemy as the forward observers' vision was obstructed by rain and jungle; fire was adjusted by sounds more than sight. They moved the 105mm concentration to within fifty yards of the Marine infantrymen.

A Japanese officer emerged from the darkness and ran toward LtCol. Walt's foxhole before fragments of a shell bursting in the trees cut him down. This was the climax of the enemy counterattack at Aogiri Ridge. The Japanese tide receded as daylight grew brighter. When the Marines moved forward at 0800, they did not find one living Japanese at Aogiri Ridge—now renamed Walt's Ridge in honor of their commander, who received the Navy Cross for his heroic leadership.

Only one Japanese stronghold in the vicinity of Walt's Ridge still survived. A supply dump along the trail linking the ridge to Hill 150. On January 11, the 1/7 Marines accompanied by two half-tracks and a platoon of light tanks eliminated the enemy resistance in four hours of fighting. It had been fifteen days of combat since the landings on December 26. It cost the division 182 killed and 640 wounded.

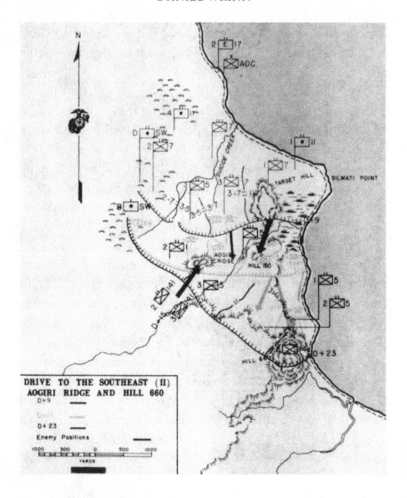

DRIVE TO THE SOUTHEAST (II)
AOGIRI RIDGE AND HILL 660

The next objective was Hill 660. It was to the left of Gen. Shepherd's zone of action and inland of the coastal track. The 3/7 Marines got orders to seize the hill. Captain Joseph W. Buckley, commander of the 7th Marines Weapons Company, created a task force to bypass Hill 660 and block the coastal trail beyond the objective.

Buckley used two platoons of infantry, a platoon of 37mm guns, two half-tracks, and two light tanks. He assigned a platoon of pioneers from the 17th Marines with the bulldozer to trail the task force. They pushed through the mud and set up a roadblock to block the line of retreat from Hill 660. The Japanese attacked with long-range, plunging fire against Capt. Buckley's task force as it advanced one mile along the trail. Because of the flat trajectory, the 37mm and 75mm guns could not destroy the enemy's automatic weapons. But the Marines succeeded in forcing enemy gunners to keep their heads down. As they advanced, Buckley's task force unreeled telephone wire to keep in contact with headquarters. Once the roadblock was in place and camouflaged, Buckley requested a truck bring in hot meals for his men. When the truck got bogged down—he sent the bulldozer to pull it free.

Buckley called in an aerial bombardment and artillery fire at 0930 on January 13. His tanks could not negotiate the ravines on the hillside. The climb became so steep that the riflemen had to sling their arms and seize handholds along the vines to pull themselves up. This is when the Japanese suddenly opened fire from trenches at the crest and pinned down the Marines climbing toward them. The Marines responded with mortar fire to silence the enemy lacking an overhead cover. Capt. Buckley's riflemen followed closely behind the mortar barrage and scattered the defenders. Many trying to escape along the coastal trail were shot down by the task force waiting for them.

Because of the torrential rain, the Japanese did not counterattack until January 16. Two companies of Katayama's troops charged up the southwestern slope and were slaughtered by small arms and mortar fire. Of the enemy lucky enough to survive and try to break through the roadblock, forty-eight perished.

After the capture of Hill 660, the nature of the campaign changed. The Allies had captured their objective and eliminated any possibility of a Japanese counterattack against the airfield. Now the Marines would repel the Japanese, who harassed the secondary beachhead at Cape Merkus. Marines would also secure the jungle-covered mountainous interior of Cape Gloucester—south of the airfields between the Yellow and Green beaches.

MOPPING UP IN THE WEST

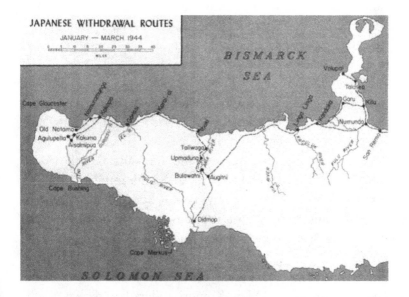

JAPANESE WITHDRAWAL ROUTES
JANUARY — MARCH 1944

THE FIGHTING at Cape Merkus on the south coast of western New Britain paled compared to Cape Gloucester's savage struggle. Japanese in the south were content to take advantage of the dense jungle and contain the 112th Cavalry on Cape Merkus. The Japanese commander, Major Komori, believed that the Allied landing force's plan was to capture an abandoned airfield at Cape Merkus. Komori built Japanese defenses to protect the airfield. He created a series of concealed bunkers with integrated fields of fire to hold the lightly armed cavalrymen in check while his troops directed harassing fire toward the beach.

The 112th Cavalry unit lacked heavy weapons. They called for 1st Marine Division tanks left behind on Finschhafen, New Guinea, because the other tanks were already turning up the mud at Cape Gloucester. Eighteen M5A1 light tanks from Company B of the 1st Marine Tank Battalion answered the call. They arrived at Cape Merkus and moved into position on January 15. The tanks attacked the next day after a squadron of Army B-24s dropped one-thousand-pound bombs on enemy jungle-covered defenses. The Marines followed up with artillery and mortars, joining in on the bombardment after two platoons of tanks and two infantry companies charged ahead.

Some tanks bogged down in the rain-soaked soil, and tank retrievers were needed to pull them free. Despite the nearly impenetrable thickets and deep mud, the tank infantry teams destroyed most of the Japanese bunkers. After eliminating the source of the harassing fire, the Allied troops pulled back. They destroyed a tank immobilized by a thrown track so the enemy could not create a pillbox. Another tank trapped in a crater was nearly destroyed—but Army engineers were able to free it and bring it back to service.

The January 16 attack broke the back of remaining Japanese resistance. Maj. Komori ordered a retreat to the vicinity of the airstrip, but the 112th Cavalry launched an attack that caught and shot them to pieces. By the time the Japanese dug in to defend the airfield—which the Americans had no intention of seizing—Komori's men lost 116 dead and 117 wounded with another 94 too sick to fight. Through starvation and sickness, the Japanese hung on until February 24, when Maj. Komori received orders to join the *Matsuda Force* in a general retreat.

On the other side of the island, after the victories at Hill 660 and Walt's Ridge, the 5th Marines focused on seizing control of the Borgen Bay shore's to the east of Yellow Beach 2. The 1/5 Marines followed the coastal trail until January 20, when the column smashed into a Japanese stronghold at Natamo Point. Documents captured earlier in the fighting described one enemy platoon supported by automatic weapons as dug in. Allied airstrikes and artillery could not suppress the enemy fire. The seized documents proved to be out of date when at least one company armed with 20mm, 37mm, and 75mm weapons stalled the Allied advance.

Marine reinforcements called in Sherman tanks that arrived in LSTs on January 23. That afternoon, supported by rocket firing DUKWs and artillery, the Marines overran Natamo Point. The battalion commander dispatched patrols along the west bank of the Natamo River. They outflanked strong enemy positions on the east bank near the stream's mouth. While the Marines executed this maneuver, the Japanese abandoned their defenses and retreated to the east.

The success at Borgen Bay and Cape Gloucester enabled the 5th Marines to probe the trails leading inward toward the village of Magairapua, where Katayama once had his headquarters. The 5th Marines led the way to trap enemy troops still bottled up on western New Britain.

Company L of the 1st Marines pursued the retreating Japanese from Cape Gloucester toward Mount Talawe. Marines crossed the mountain's eastern slope and weaved their way through a cluster of lesser outcroppings, through Mount Langila and into the saddle between Mounts Tangi and Talawe. They discovered four unoccupied bunkers situated to defend the track they'd followed, with another trail running east to west. Company L found the main route on the coast to the village of Agulupella from Sag Sag and ultimately onto Natamo Point on the northern coast.

Taking full advantage of this discovery, the 1st Marine patrol advanced south along the trail. At the same time, a composite company from the 7th Marines landed at Sag Sag on the West Coast and moved along an east-west track. Australian reserve officer, William Weidman, a former Episcopal missionary at Sag Sag, served as guide and contact for the natives. When enemy resistance stopped the 1st Marine patrol short of the trail junction near Mount Talawe, Company K of the 1st Marines attacked.

For three hours, the Marines of Company K tried to break through a line of bunkers concealed by jungle growth. The Marines took fifteen casualties and withdrew beyond the reach of the Japanese mortars. The Japanese broke from cover and pursued a brave but foolish move that exposed the enemy troops to a deadly fire. This vigorous pursuit along the coast and the inland trails failed to trap the Japanese. The Marines captured Gen. Matsuda's abandoned headquarters in the shadow of Mount Talawe. Inside they found documents buried instead of burned—possibly because the smoke would bring down artillery fire or airstrikes. The Japanese general and his troops escaped.

Gen. Shepherd believed that Matsuda was headed to the vicinity of Mount Talawe to the south. He organized a battalion of six rifle companies—nearly four thousand men—entrusted to Chesty Puller. This patrol would advance from Agulupella on the east-west track down to Government Trail. Then all the way to Gilnit, a village on the Itni River, inland of Cape Bushing on the southern New Britain coast. Before LtCol. Puller could advance, the intelligence section discovered that the enemy was retreating to the northeast toward

Rabaul. Gen. Shepherd detached the newly arrived 1/5 Marines. He reduced LtCol. Puller's force from almost 4,000 to 350 Marines for the jungle march to Gilnit.

During this trek, Puller's Marines depended on supplies dropped from Allied planes. Puller was also assigned 150 native bearers to carry rations and supplies. Air Force B-17s dropped tons of cargo. The patrol was only possible because of the supplies dropped from the sky. But this did little to ease the Marine discomfort of plodding through the mud.

Despite the air assistance, the march to Gilnit taxed Marine ingenuity and hardened them for future action. LtCol. Puller, who had led many patrols during the American intervention in Nicaragua, seemed in good spirits during this action. Division supply clerks, aware of Pullers' disdain for any creature comforts, were startled when they read his requisitions for hundreds of insect repellent bottles. Puller later wrote:

We were always soaked and everything we owned was likewise, and that lotion made the best damn stuff to start a fire with that you ever saw.

LtCol. Puller's Marines slogged toward Gilnit on the Itni River, killing seventy-five Japanese, capturing one straggler, and weapons and equipment odds and ends. One abandoned enemy pack contained an American flag, probably captured by a *141st Infantry* soldier during Japan's Philippine conquest. When the patrol reached Gilnit, they met no opposition. Puller's Marines made contact with an rmy patrol from Cape Merkus and then headed toward the northern coast on February 16.

On February 12, to the west, Company B of the 1st Marines boarded landing craft to cross the Dampier Strait to occupy Rooke Island, fifteen miles off the coast of New Britain. Division intelligence believed that the enemy garrison had departed. They were correct. The enemy withdrawal began on December 6, three weeks before the Cape Gloucester landings.

Colonel Sato and half of his *51st Reconnaissance Regiment* of 500 men sailed to Cape Bushing, where Sato led his command up the river and joined the main body of the *Matsuda Force* east of Mount Talawe. Instead of committing Sato's troops to the defense of Hill 660, Matsuda directed him to delay and harass the 1st and 5th Marines who converged on the inland trail net. Col. Sato succeeded in stalling the Marine patrols. He bought time for Matsuda's forces to retreat to the northern coasts with the *51st Reconnaissance Regiment* serving as the rearguard.

Once the Marines realized what Gen. Matsuda was up to, cutting their line of retreat became the highest priority. They withdrew the 1/5 Marines from the Puller patrol on the eve of the march toward Gilnit. On February 3, Gen. Shepherd realized the Japanese did not have the strength to mount a counterattack on the airfields and devoted all his resources to destroy retreating enemy troops. Shepherd chose the 5th Marines, now restored to three-battalion strength, to pursue the fleeing Japanese troops. While light aircraft scouted the coastal track, landing craft stood fast and waited to debark the regiment to cut off and destroy Gen. Matsuda's force. Bad weather stalled the 5th Marines. Clouds concealed the enemy from aerial observation while the boiling surf ruled out landings on several beaches. With over 5,000 Marines and Army troops, the Allies rotated their battalions and sent out fresh troops each day. They also used ten LCMs (Landing Craft, Mechanical) to leapfrog the retreating Japanese.

Marines were not called upon to make marches for more than two days in a row, with few exceptions. After a one day hike, they either remained at camp for three days or made the next jump by LCM. The 5th Marines expected a battle for the Japanese supply point at Iboki Point, but enemy troops dwindled. Instead of encountering resistance by a resolute and clever rearguard, the 5th Marines only found stragglers, most wounded or too sick to fight. Marines kept up pressure on retreating Japanese troops. On February 24, they took Iboki Point without loss or even one man wounded.

During this action, American amphibious forces seized Eniwetok and Kwajalein Atolls in the Marshall Islands. The Central Pacific offensive now gathered momentum. Allied carrier strikes proved Truk was too vulnerable to continue serving as a significant enemy naval base. Now conscious of the threat to their inner perimeter developing to the north, the Japanese pulled back the fleet units from Truk and aircraft from Rabaul. On February 19, two days after the Allies invaded Eniwetok, enemy fighters at Rabaul took off to challenge an American air raid. When the Japanese bombers returned the next day, not a single operational Japanese fighter remained at the airfields.

The defense of Rabaul now depended on ground forces. LtGen. Sakai, commander of the *17th Division*, received orders to not dig in near Cape Hoskins and instead move to Rabaul. Sakai assumed the supplies he'd positioned along the trail would enable at least the most spirited of Matsuda's troops to stay ahead of the Marines and reach the fortress.

What was left of the self-propelled barges could carry the remaining troops and heavy equipment needed to defend Rabaul. This retreat would be an ordeal for the Japanese. The 5th Marines had already showed how swiftly they could move by taking advantage of Allied controlled skies and coastal waters. A full two-week march separated the nearest of Matsuda soldiers from their destination. While attrition was heavy, those who could contribute the least to Rabaul's defenses fell by the wayside.

LANDINGS AT VOLUPAI

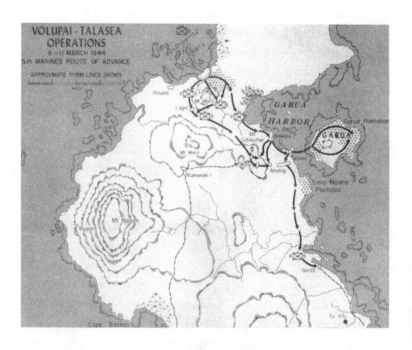

MARCH 6 WAS D-Day for the 5th Marines to land on the west coast of the Willaumez Peninsula—halfway between the base and the tip. Division intelligence believed that the Japanese strength between Talasea, site of the crude airstrip, and Cape

Hoskins, across Kimbe Bay were equal to the 5th Marines. Still, most of the enemy troops were defending Cape Hoskins. If the intelligence estimates were correct, Sakai prepared the last defense of Cape Hoskins before ordered to retreat to Rabaul.

A torpedo boat landed a recon team at Bagum. Their orders were to discover the intent of Japanese preparations near Volupai, nine miles from Red Beach, chosen for the assault. They learned Red Beach was lightly defended from native sources who'd worked at a plantation operated in the area before the war. The natives confirmed the Marine estimates of an enemy force of 600 men, two-thirds of them near Talasea, armed with artillery and mortars.

The Royal Australian Air Force, based out of Kiriwina Island to the south, bombed the Volupai region for three days. A force of 5th Marines, designated as Landing Team A, loaded into a small flotilla of landing craft set out from Iboki Point with an escort of torpedo boats.

On March 6, at 0835, the first amphibian tractors carrying assault troops clawed their way onto Red Beach. Sherman tanks in Army LCMs opened fire with machine guns. They waited to direct their 75mm weapons against any enemy gunner opposing the Allied landing force. Aside from difficult-to-pinpoint small arms fire, enemy opposition consisted mainly of mortar barrages, screened by the terrain. As Japanese mortar shells burst among the approaching landing craft, Captain Theodore A. Petras, flying a Piper L-4 Grasshopper, dove low over mortar positions and dropped hand grenades from the cockpit. Natives warned the Allied assault forces of a machine gun nest dominating the beach from the slopes on Little Mount Worri. The 1/5 Marines leading the way found it abandoned and encountered no serious opposition as they dug into protect the beachhead.

Four Sherman's supported the 5th Marines as they pushed farther inland, pressing their attack. One of the medium tanks got bogged down on Red Beach's soft sand, but the other three continued in a line. The lead tank lost momentum on a muddy rise, and two Japanese soldiers carrying landmines surged from cover to attack. Company E rifleman cut one down, but the other detonated his mine against the tank, killing himself and a Marine trying to stop him. The explosion jammed the tank's turret and stunned the crewmen inside, shaken but not wounded. The damaged Sherman moved aside to allow the other two tanks to pass, returning to the trail only to hit another mine.

After losing two tanks, one temporarily immobilized, and the other permanently out of action, the 5th Marines continued their advance. During the fighting at a Volupai coconut plantation, a dead Japanese soldier's body had a map showing the enemy positions around Talasea. By early afternoon, regimental intelligence distributed the information, which proved valuable for future operations.

Company E of the 5th Marines followed the trail to the plantation. At the same time, Company G kept pace, crossing the western shoulder of Little Mount Worri. Five P-39s from Airfield No. 2 at Cape Gloucester supported the attack. The pilots could not pinpoint the troops below and instead bombed Cape Hoskins, where there was no danger of hitting any Marines. Even without the aerial attack, the 2/5 Marines overran the plantation by nightfall and dug in for the night. Marines counted thirty-five Japanese killed.

Throughout the fighting, Combat Team A took eighty-four casualties. The artillery batteries suffered a more significant number of casualties than rifle companies.

The 2/11 Marines set up their 75mm howitzers on the open beach—exposed to fire from the 90mm mortars, which Capt. Petras showered with hand grenades. Some of the Navy Corpsmen on Red Beach, who helped the wounded artillerymen, ended up as casualties themselves. Thirty-four of the Marines killed and wounded on March 6 were members of the artillery unit. The gunners succeeded in registering their fires that afternoon and harassing the enemy through the night.

While the Marines prepared to renew their attack on the next day, the Japanese opposed them in order to keep a line of retreat open for the *Matsuda Force*. By doing so, the Japanese fell back from their prepared positions on the fringes of the Volupai plantation. This included the mortar pits that had caused such havoc with the 2/11 Marines. They dug in on the northern slopes of Mount Schleuther, overlooking the trail leading from the plantation to Bitokara village on the coast. Company F was sent uphill to disrupt the Japanese plan, while Company E remained on the trail to build up a base of fire.

On the right flank, Company F, the weapons platoon, surged from the undergrowth. They surprised Japanese machine gunners setting up their weapon, killing them, and turning the gun against the enemy troops. Company F's advance caught the Japanese in mid deployment and drove them back, killing over forty of their men. The 5th Marines established a night perimeter that extended from Mount Schleuther to the trail and embraced a portion of both.

The March 7 action was a departure from the plan. Originally, the 3/5 Marines would assume responsibility for the beachhead. Landing craft that had carried assault troops would depart from Red Beach on D-Day, and pick up the 3rd Battalion at Iboki Point, bringing them to Volupai. If the reinforcements were to arrive in time for an attack on the morning of March 7, this would require a dangerous nighttime Volupai approach through uncharted waters studded with sharp coral that could tear open the hull of the landing craft.

Gen. Shepherd decided the risks of such a move outweighed the advantages and canceled it at the last moment. No boats started the return voyage to Red Beach until after daylight on March 7, delaying Marine reinforcements until late afternoon. This left the 1st Battalion with only enough time to send Company C a short distance inland on the trail to the village of Liappo. When the trail petered out among trees and vines, Marines hacked their way forward until they ran out of daylight short of their objective.

The 1/5 Marines resumed the advance on March 8. Companies A and B moved through parallel paths leading east of Little Mount Worri.

Company A Marines peered through dense undergrowth and saw a figure in a Japanese uniform and opened fire. This man was a native wearing clothing discarded by the enemy and serving as a guide for Company B. The shots triggered an exchange of fire that killed two Marines, wounded the guide, and several others. Afterward, the advance resumed, but through formidable terrain—muddy ravines choked with brush and vines—which slowed the Marines as darkness fell with the battalion still on the trail.

The 2nd Battalion probed deeper into the enemy defenses. Patrols pushed ahead on the morning of March 8. They found Japanese troops dug in at the Bitokara Mission. The enemy fell back before the Marines could charge their position. Marines occupied Bitokara and advanced as far as Talasea taking over the abandoned airstrip. Other Marine patrols climbed the steep slopes of Mount Schleuther and collided with the enemy troops. Fire from a 90mm mortar, 75mm gun, and small arms killed eighteen Marines. Rather than press the attack in the darkness, Marines withdrew from the mountain and dug in at the Bitokara Mission. Mortars and artillery hammered the defenses through the night, leaving one company to defend the Talasea airstrip.

On the morning of March 9, Company G of the 2nd Marine Battalion advanced up Mount Schleuther while companies B and C cleared villages around the base. Company G expected to meet strong opposition during its part of the coordinated attack. But the Japanese had withdrawn from the mountaintop and left behind one artillery piece, two stragglers, and three dead. Enemy troops had festooned the abandoned 75mm gun with vines serving as tripwires for a booby-trap. When Marines hacked at the vines to examine the weapon more closely, they released the firing pins and detonated a round in the chamber. Since the Japanese gun crew had plugged the bore before they fled, the explosion ruptured the breach block and wounded several Marines.

After yielding the dominant terrain, the Japanese chose not to defend any of the villages clustered at the mountain's base. This opened up a route for the 5th Marines across the Willaumez Peninsula to support further operations against Gen. Matsuda's line of retreat. Since the March 6 offensive, the Allied force had killed an estimated 150 Japanese at the cost of seventeen dead and 114 wounded, most casualties taking place on the first day. The last phase of the fighting that began on Red Beach consisted of securing Garua Island, abandoned by the Japanese.

Results of the action at the base of the Willaumez Peninsula were mixed. The grassy Talasea airstrip lacked enough length to accommodate fighter planes. Still, the division's liaison planes made widespread use of it, landing on either side of a Japanese aircraft's carcass until the wreckage could be hauled away. The trail net was a web of muddy paths that required long hours of hard work by Company F of the 17th Marines. Army engineers used a 10-ton wrecker to recover three Sherman tanks that had become mired during the fighting. By March 10, the trails could support a further advance. Two days later, the 3/5 Marines provided a guard of honor. The same American flag flown over Airfield No. 2 on Cape Gloucester was raised over Bitokara.

FINAL COMBAT AND RELIEF

THE ALLIED FLOTILLA of Navy LCTs and Army LCMs supporting the Volupai landings continued to inflict damage on Japanese coastal traffic. On March 9, landing crafts carrying supplies around the tip of the peninsula spotted four enemy barges. They were beached and carelessly camouflaged. An LCT opened fire from its 20mm cannon and destroyed one of the Japanese barges. After that, two Army LCMs used their 37mm guns and opened fire on another barge beached on the shore.

The Japanese tried to make the best use of their shrinking number of barges, but the bulk of Gen. Matsuda's troops moved overland. A hundred Japanese were dug in at Garilli, but by the time Company K of the 3/5 Marines attacked on March 11, the Japanese had withdrawn to a new trail three miles away. Marines fought a series of actions lasting four days. The Japanese retreated a few hundred yards, dragging their 75mm gun that anchored each of the blocking positions. On March 16, Company K received 81mm mortars from an arriving LCM. The enemy turned their cannon seaward to deal with the threat but could not hit the landing craft. After the Marine mortars landed, they were quickly put into action. Japanese troops again withdrew, but this time they faded away since the bulk of Gen. Matsuda's force had escaped eastward.

The 5th Marines dispatched patrols southbound to the base of the Willaumez Peninsula, only capturing an occasional straggler, confirming the departure of Gen. Matsuda's primary force. The 1st Marine Division established training sites, a comfortable headquarters, and a hospital that used Japanese medicine stocks. Marines could swim in a rest area off the Garua beaches and hot springs ashore. The Navy then built a base on the Willaumez Peninsula for torpedo boats to harass surviving Japanese barges. On March 27, only the second day after the base was operating, Allied aircraft mistook two boats for enemy craft. They attacked—killing five and wounding eighteen sailors with friendly fire.

At the new training center on Garua, classes were taught to produce amphibious scouts for future operations. Headquarters decided that a reconnaissance of Cape Hoskins would be a suitable graduation exercise since aerial observers had seen no sign of enemy there. On April 13, sixteen trainees, two native guides, and a rifle platoon from the 2/5 Marines embarked on a pair of LCMs to Cape Hoskins. Two instructors stood by in one landing craft as the platoon established a trail block. Future scouts advanced toward the airfield at Cape Hoskins. The patrol encountered small arms and mortar fire en route to their objective. But the Marines had learned their lessons well, and they broke off the action and escaped with no casualties.

The Japanese had retreated. Maj. Komori's troops blazed the trail for Sato's command from Augitni to the northern coast. They encountered a dispiriting number of hungry stragglers as they marched toward Kandoka, a supply depot ten miles west of the Willaumez Peninsula. Komori's troops came under fire from an American landing craft as they crossed the Kuhu River. The rain-swollen river was a serious obstacle and became a detour that lasted two days until reaching a point where the stream narrowed.

On March 17, Komori's provisions ran out, forcing his troops to survive on birds, fish, and taro root, supplemented by coconuts from a nearby plantation. After losing a dozen men and additional time crossing the river, Komori's troops struggled into Kandoka. Only to discover that the food and other supplies had already been carried off to Rabaul. Maj. Komori pressed on through this crushing disappointment. His men continued to live off the land as best they could. Another five Japanese troops drowned in the fast-moving Kuhu River, and a native hired guide defected. Maj. Komori came down with a severe bout of malaria, and although physically weakened, he forced himself to continue.

Japanese survivors strived onward toward Cape Hoskins and ultimately into Rabaul. On Easter Sunday, 1944, a handful of half-starved enemy troops wandered onto the San

Remo Plantation, where Marines had bivouacked after pursuing Japanese troops eastward from the Willaumez Peninsula. The Marine unit was preparing to pass in review for the regimental commander when a sentry saw them and opened fire. The ensuing firefight killed three Japanese. One of the dead was Maj. Komori. In his pack was a rusty revolver and a diary that described the suffering of his command.

Col. Sato took the rest of the rearguard intended for the *Matsuda Force* and set out from Augitni on March 7. One day after Maj. Komori had sent word on the nineteenth that the 5th Marines' patrols had fanned out from the Willaumez Peninsula, where the reinforced regiment had landed two weeks earlier. When Sato reached Linga Linga he came across an abandoned Marine patrol bivouac. Sato's force had shrunk to less than 250 men, half the number he had starting out.

The following day, he was shocked when Allied landing craft appeared as his men prepared to cross the Kapaluk River. Sato set up a perimeter to repel the expected attack. The boats carried elements of the 2/1 Marines and landed a patrol from Company F on a beach beyond Kandoka. Another platoon was dispatched westward along the coastal track. Col. Sato was only aware of the landing's general location and groped eastward toward the village. On March 26, they collided. The Japanese surprised the Marines crossing a small stream and pinned them down for three hours until Company F reinforcements forced the Japanese to break off, take to the jungle, and bypass Kandoka.

Col. Sato's column disappeared into the jungle. One of the division's light airplanes scouting landing sites for the battalion sited the end of the column near Linga Linga. The Piper L-4 Grasshopper pilot sketched where the Japanese were and dropped the map to one of the troop-laden landing craft. The pilot then led the way to an undefended beach where the Marines waded ashore and set out to pursue Col. Sato and his troops. On March 30, an eight-man Marine patrol spotted a pair of Japanese with their rifles slung. These enemy troops were members of a seventy-three man patrol—too many to handle.

After the enemy column moved off, the eight-man patrol hurried back to Kandoka and reported. Outfitted with more machine guns, mortars, and men. This reinforced rifle platoon returned to the trail. The Japanese encountered another Marine patrol, which took up a position on high ground commanding the trail. When the reinforced rifle platoon heard gunfire, they hurried to aid the other Marines. The resulting slaughter killed fifty-five Japanese troops, including Col. Sato, who died, sword in hand, charging Marines. The Marines did not suffer one casualty during this encounter.

On April 9, the 3/1 Marines continued to search for enemy stragglers. The bulk of Gen. Matsuda's force, and whatever supplies it could transport, had retreated to Cape Hoskins.

Army troops were taking over for the Marines. It had now been four months since the landing at Cape Gloucester. The time had come for the amphibious forces to move on to an operation that would make better use of their specialized equipment and training. The last Marine action took place on April 22, when an ambush, sprung by the 2/5 Marines, killed twenty Japanese and caused the campaign's last Marine fatality. By seizing western New Britain as part of Rabaul's isolation, the division suffered 1,083 wounded and 310 killed in action—one-fourth of the Japanese casualties.

The capture of the Cape Gloucester airfields in early February 1944 tied down the 1st Marine Division for an extended period. This alarmed the recently appointed Commandant of the Marine Corps, Gen. Vandegrift. Referring to an extended engagement in New Britain, he wrote:

Six months there, and [the 1st Marine Division] will no longer be a well-trained amphibious division.

Vandegrift urged US Fleet Admiral Earnest King to help him pry the division from General Douglas MacArthur's grasp so he could again engage in amphibious operations. Admiral Nimitz, the commander-in-chief of Pacific Ocean Areas, requested the 1st Marine Division for the Palau Islands' impending invasion. The capture would protect MacArthur's flank on his advance to the Philippines.

Adm. Nimitz made the Army's 140th Infantry Division available to MacArthur. He swapped a division capable of taking over the New Britain Campaign for one that could spearhead the amphibious offensive against Japan. MacArthur briefly kept control of one Marine division, Company A, 1st Tank Battalion. The unit's medium tanks landed on April 22 at Hollandia on the northern coast of New Guinea. A swamp behind the beachhead stopped the Shermans from assisting the inland advance.

The commanding general of the Army's 140th Infantry Division was Major General Isaac R. Brush. He arrived on April 10 and arranged for the relief. His advance echelon landed on the 23rd, with the rest of the division following five days after. The 1st Marine Division departed on April 6 and May 4. They left behind the 12th Defense Battalion, who continued to provide antiaircraft defense for the Cape Gloucester airfields until replaced by an Army unit later in May.

The 1st Marine Division had plunged into an unforgiving jungle and overwhelmed a resolute enemy. They captured the Cape Gloucester airfields and drove the Japanese from western New Britain in just over four months. Several factors helped the Marines defeat the Japanese. The Allied control of the air and sea provided mobility. It disrupted the coastal barge traffic, which the enemy depended on for the movement of large quantities of medicine and supplies desperately needed for the retreat to Rabaul. Landing craft armed with rockets, aided by tanks and rocket-equipped amphibian trucks fired from landing craft, helped support the landings. But the size of the island and the lack of fixed coastal defenses reduced the efficiency of naval gunfire.

Marines defied the swamp and undergrowth by using superior engineering skills and bringing forward tanks that crushed enemy emplacements—adding to formidable American firepower. Through photo analysis, an art that improved rapidly, the Americans misinterpreted the nature of the swamp forest. However, Marine intelligence made excellent use of captured Japanese documents throughout the campaign. But it was the courage and endurance of the average Marine who made victory possible on Cape Gloucester. A Marine braved discomfort, disease, and violent death during his time in this hellish green Inferno.

MACARTHUR'S MARINES

GENERAL MACARTHUR WAS desperate for a trained amphibious unit to capture Rabaul. While the 1st Division Marines finished their rehabilitation in Australia, MacArthur approached the commander of the 6th Army, Lieutenant General Walter Kruger. MacArthur wanted to seize Rabaul and break the back of the Japanese resistance in the area. Worried about air cover for his amphibious operations, MacArthur planned to use the 1st Division Marines to capture the Cape Gloucester airfields. Allied aircraft based out of the captured airfields would support the 1st Division Marines assault on Rabaul.

The initial operational concept called for the conquest of western New Britain by storming Rabaul. He would split the 1st Marine Division by sending Combat Team A (5th Marines) against Gasmata on the island's southern coast. Combat team C (7th Marines) would seize the beachhead near the principal objective at Cape Gloucester's airfields. This would enable the Army's 503rd Parachute Infantry to exploit the Cape Gloucester beachhead. Combat Team B (1st Marines) would be held in reserve.

But revisions came swiftly in late October 1943. The new plan now did not mention the capture of Rabaul. MajGen. Rupertus protested splitting Combat Team C. LtGen. Kruger decided to use all three battalions for the primary assault, substituting a battalion from Combat Team B for the West Coast landings. The airborne landing at Cape Gloucester would remain in the plan. But MajGen. Rupertus warned that foul weather could delay the drop and jeopardize Marine battalions already fighting ashore. This altered version earmarked Army troops for the landing on the southern coast.

Kruger's staff shifted the site from Gasmata to Arawe, a location closer to Allied airfields and farther from Rabaul's troops and aircraft. Combat Team B would put one battalion ashore southwest of the airfields. Two battalions of the 1st Marines would follow up on the assault at Cape Gloucester with Combat Team C. This left the division reserve, Combat Team A, to employ elements of the 5th Marines and reinforce the Cape Gloucester landings or conduct operations against the offshore islands to the west of New Britain.

During a December 14 briefing, only one day before the landings at Arawe, Gen. MacArthur asked how the Marines felt about the maneuver at Cape Gloucester. The division operations officer, Colonel Edwin A. Pollock, saw this opportunity to declare that the Marines objected to the plan. It depended on a speedy advance inland by a single reinforced regiment. To prevent heavy losses among the lightly armored paratroops, Pollock believed it would be better to bolster the amphibious forces than to try for an aerial envelopment that might fail or be delayed by the weather.

While he made no comment at the time, MacArthur may have heeded what Pollock said. Whatever the reason was, Kruger's staff eliminated the airborne portion and instructed the two battalions of the 1st Marines, still with Combat Team B, to land immediately after the assault waves. This would sustain the momentum of their attack and alert the division reserve to provide further reinforcements.

MAJOR GENERAL WILLIAM RUPERTUS

BORN ON NOVEMBER 14, 1889, in Washington DC, Rupertus's military career began in the District of Columbia National Guard. In 1910, he became a cadet in the US Revenue Cutter Service School, the Coast Guard Academy, in New London, Connecticut.

After being commissioned as a second lieutenant in the United States Marine Corps, he attended officer school and graduated first in his class in 1915. He commanded a Marine detachment aboard the USS Florida in World War I as a first lieutenant. After the war, he was promoted to captain and assigned to Haiti, where he gained experience in jungle fighting tactics.

He spent a year in the Army Command and General Staff School in Fort Leavenworth, Kansas. He was one of three Marines selected for that year and graduated with distinction. In 1929, he was given his first Far East assignment in Peking, China, and was promoted to major. Peking was quiet at the time, and while on duty, his first wife and two children died from a scarlet fever epidemic.

He returned to the War Plans Section at Headquarters in 1936 where he was appointed Chief of Staff of the Fleet Marine Force. After four years of service stateside, he returned to Shanghai, China as Executive Officer of the 4th Marines. There he became a lieutenant colonel. He witnessed the Japanese's brutal methods as they attempted to take over the International Settlement. Only with patience and discipline was a clash averted with the Japanese at that time.

After returning from China, Rupertus took command of the Marine Barracks in Washington DC, Guantánamo Bay, Cuba, and San Diego, California.

At the war's outbreak, Brigadier General Rupertus was the 1st Marine Division's assistant commander, training in New River, North Carolina, under Gen. Vandegrift. When the 1st Division opened the Allied offensive in the Pacific, landing on the Solomons on August 7, 1942, Rupertus was an assistant division commander and led a successful attack on Tulagi, Gavutu, and the Tanambogo Islands. Two months later, at a ceremony on Guadalcanal, Adm. Nimitz awarded him the Navy Cross for his leadership in the seizure of those islands. Part of his citation read:

For exposing himself frequently and fearlessly to enemy fire and for setting an outstanding example of calmness and courage.

In 1943, when Gen. Vandegrift assumed command of the newly created 1st Marine Amphibious Corps, Gen. Rupertus took command of the 1st Division Marines. He brought a firsthand, thorough knowledge of operations in the Southwest Pacific. In a string of brilliant victories from December 28, 1943, to April 1944, which involved many secondary amphibious operations and bloody battles, the 1st Marine Division, under his leadership, cleared the western part of New Britain and drove the enemy back to Rabaul.

During the Cape Gloucester operations, his careful use of Marine scouts and air maps allowed ground troops to take a nearly undefended route to the Cape Gloucester airfields. After the campaign, Gen. MacArthur went ashore to personally thank Rupertus for the valor of his division and awarded him the Army's distinguished service medal for "exceptionally meritorious and distinguished service during an undertaking fraught with hazard." Part of his citation read:

Gen. Rupertus overcame great difficulties of weather and terrain. After firmly establishing a beachhead between two large enemy forces, he brilliantly maneuvered his troops to destroy each other in turn. While the stubbornly resisting enemy had every advantage of terrain and established offenses, he inflicted on it disproportionate losses of a 10 to 1 ratio. The skillful and courageous leadership of Gen. Rupertus was largely responsible for the success of this bold extension of our operations.

In November 1944, after the Peleliu Campaign, he returned to the US. He was appointed the Commandant of the Marine Corps School in Quantico, Virginia.

He died of a heart attack on March 25, 1945 and was buried at Arlington National Cemetery among family members.

LIEUTENANT COLONEL LEWIS WALT

Lewis William Walt, "Lew Walt," was born on February 16, 1913, in Wabaunsee County, Kansas. Walt graduated from

Colorado State University in 1936 with a degree in chemistry. After graduation, he was commissioned as a second lieutenant in the Army Field Artillery Reserve. He resigned that commission to accept an appointment as a Marine second lieutenant on July 6, 1936.

After Lieut. Walt completed The Basic School at Philadelphia in April 1937, he was assigned to the 6th Marine Regiment in San Diego, California, as a machine-gun platoon leader. He embarked for China in August 1937, where he took part in defense of Shanghai's International Settlement until February 1938, when he returned to San Diego. In June 1939, he began his second overseas tour when he was assigned to the Marine Barracks on Guam in the Mariana Islands. Here he was promoted to first lieutenant in October 1939.

After returning to the US in June 1941, before the entry into World War II, Lieut. Walt was assigned as a company commander in the Officer Candidates Class at the Marine Corps School in Quantico, Virginia. Here he was promoted to captain.

In early 1942, Captain Walt volunteered to join the 1st Marine Raider Battalion and was stationed with the battalion on Samoa. On August 7, 1942, as commander of Company A, 1st Raider Battalion, he landed his company on Tulagi for the assault in the British Solomon Islands. He was awarded the Silver Star for his conspicuous gallantry during this landing. After the action, he joined the 5th Marines on Guadalcanal, where he took part in combat as Commanding Officer of the 2/5 Marines. He was promoted to major in September 1942.

In October 1942, Major Walt was wounded in action but continued to fight. Two months later, he was promoted to lieutenant colonel, on the spot, for his distinguished leadership and gallantry in action during the Guadalcanal Campaign.

Following hospitalization and rehabilitation in Australia, LtCol. Walt led the 2/5 Marines in the assault on Cape

Gloucester. In the middle of the campaign, he was ordered to take command of the 3/5 Marines during an intense battle for Aogiri Ridge. He earned his first Navy Cross during this action, and Aogiri Ridge was renamed "Walt's Ridge" by Gen. Shepherd. After leaving Cape Gloucester in late February 1944, LtCol. Walt was ordered to the Naval Hospital in Oakland, California, to treat his malaria.

In June 1944, he returned to action in the Pacific Theater. That September, he landed with the Marine force on Peleliu as Regimental Executive Officer of the 5th Marines. On the first day of the battle, he was again ordered to command the 3/5 Marines after the battalion's CO and XO were wounded. After dark on the first day of fighting, three battalion companies had failed to contact the command post, and their whereabouts were unknown. At significant risk to himself, LtCol. Walt went into enemy territory in the middle of the night and located the missing companies. He directed them to their correct position along the divisional line. For these actions, LtCol. Walt was awarded his second Navy Cross.

In November 1944, Walt returned to the US and assumed duty as Chief of the Marine Officer Candidates' School Tactics Section.

Gen. Walt died at 76 years old on March 26, 1989, in Gulfport, Mississippi. He was buried in Quantico National Cemetery.

GARAND M-1 RIFLE

AFTER THE GUADALCANAL CAMPAIGN, the 1st Marine Division received the M-1 rifle. This new rifle was designed by John Garand, a civilian employee from the Springfield Armory in Massachusetts. This weapon was semiautomatic, gas-operated, and weighed 9.5 pounds with an eight-round clip. While less accurate at a longer range than the former standard rifle, the M-1903, which Marine snipers continued to use, the M-1 Garand could lay down a deadly volume of fire at a short range typical to jungle warfare.

The M-1 used a .30-06 round and was the first semiautomatic rifle to be generally issued to any nation's infantry. In November 1941, the Marine Corps classified the M-1 as its standard service rifle. Its bayonet was an M-1905 bayonet. Several Marines resisted the Garand at first because they had become used to the Springfield rifle for almost 30 years. The Springfield was well-respected because of its long-range accuracy and reliability under the harshest of battlefield conditions.

The M-1 Garand gave Marine riflemen a superior firepower advantage against the Japanese opponent, who carried Arisaka Type 99s, which were among the best bolt-action rifles of the war.

Reliable and easy to maintain in the field, an M-1-equipped Marine rifle platoon could sustain the same volume of fire as a full company armed with bolt-action rifles. Operation of the M-1 was simple. Ammo loaded with an eight-round clip inserted into the top of the receiver. When the rifleman fired his last round, the bolt locked to the rear, and the empty clip ejected with a unique *ping*. Reloading, the rifleman simply pushed another loaded clip into the top of the receiver. Once the clip was fully inserted, it unlocked the bolt which stripped off the first round to load in the chamber.

A common problem experienced by new shooters was known as the "M-1 thumb," which happened when the rifleman failed to quickly take his thumb off the clip as he loaded. When the bolt unlocked, it could smash a shooter's thumb against the front of the ejection port. This usually only happened once for most new shooters. While the M-1 had some minor deficiencies, it was without question the finest service rifle of World War II. Marines who carried it in combat swore by its reliability, simplicity, and hard-hitting firepower. It served the Marine Corps well in Korea and through many years of the Cold War until retired from service in the early 1960s.

PIPER L-4 GRASSHOPPER

THE 1ST MARINE Division had an air force of their own at Cape Gloucester. It consisted of a dozen Piper L-4 Grasshoppers provided by the Army. This improvised air force could trace its origins back to the summer of 1943, before the division plunged into the hellish inferno on New Britain.

Captain Petras was Gen. Vandegrift's personal pilot. He devised a plan that would acquire light aircraft for artillery spotting. Gen. Rupertus had seen the Army troops making use of the Piper Grasshoppers on maneuvers. He presented the plan to Gen. MacArthur, who promised to give the 1st Marine Division twelve Piper Grasshoppers for their next operation.

When the 1st Marine Division arrived off the southwestern tip of New Guinea to prepare for further combat, Gen. Rupertus directed Petras to organize an aviation unit from among the Marines. The call went out for volunteers with aviation experience. Out of sixty candidates, twelve were qualified as pilots in the new Air Liaison Unit. When the dozen Piper L-4 Grasshoppers arrived as promised, six proved to be in excellent condition while three needed repairs. The remaining three were only fit to provide parts to keep the others flying.

Nine flyable planes practiced a variety of tasks during the two months of training. Afterward, airmen gained experience in radio communications, artillery spotting, and snagging messages hung in a container trailing a pennant to help the pilot see it from a line strung between two poles.

The division's air force landed at Cape Gloucester from LSTs on D-Day. After reassembling the aircraft, they were put into action. The radios installed in the Piper Grasshoppers were too balky for artillery spotting. The pilots concentrated on courier flights, photographic reconnaissance, and delivering small amounts of cargo.

Piper Grasshoppers could drop a case of dry rations with pinpoint accuracy from an altitude of 200 feet. These light planes could also become attack aircraft when pilots or observers rained hand grenades onto enemy positions.

The Piper L-4 Grasshopper evolved from the civilian plane the Piper J-3 Cub, which was the name most military personnel referred to it as. The only differences were the paint color, and more windows for better visibility. Mechanically, however, they were one and the same. There was room for a pilot in front and a spotter and radio in back, who could perform reconnaissance duties, looking out the extended windows.

The Piper L-4 Grasshopper was not armed, nor armored, which made it vulnerable to antiaircraft guns, but allowed it to fly at low altitudes and low speeds, giving it ideal maneuverability for observation and transportation of supplies and information. It was used in both the Pacific and European Theaters.

FORTRESS OF RABAUL

At Simpson Harbor on the northeastern tip of New Britain, Rabaul served as a naval and air base. It was also a troop staging area for Japanese conquests in New Guinea and the Solomon Islands.

Shortly after the attack on Pearl Harbor, Rabaul was captured by thousands of Japanese naval landing forces. Once the Japanese had seized Rabaul, they got to work converting it into a significant installation. They improved the harbor facilities and built barracks and airfields. They brought in hundreds of thousands of soldiers, airmen, and sailors, who either passed through the base en route to operations elsewhere or stayed to defend it. The Japanese Army dug hundreds of kilometers of tunnels to shelter from Allied air attacks. They also expanded the facilities by constructing Army barracks and support structures. By 1943 there were over 110,000 troops based on Rabaul.

After MacArthur escaped from the Philippines and assumed command of the Southwest Pacific Area, Rabaul became his dominant objective. MacArthur proposed a two-pronged advance on the fortress, bombing it from the air while amphibious forces closed in through eastern New Britain and the Solomon Islands.

When the Allies began to close their pincers on Rabaul, the strategy changed. Through MacArthur's opposition, the American Joint Chiefs decided to bypass the stronghold. As a result, Rabaul remained in Japanese hands for the rest of the war, though the Allies controlled the rest of New Britain.

THE JUNGLE BATTLEFIELD

THROUGHOUT THE CAMPAIGN, the 1st Marine Division fought the terrain, weather, and an unyielding Japanese enemy. Seasonal monsoon rains fell with the velocity of a firehose, soaking everyone, sending streams from their banks, and turning trails into muddy quagmires. The volcanic island terrain varied from coastal plain to mountains that rose as high as 7,000 feet above sea level. The forest-covered island was punctuated by grasslands, large coconut plantations, and garden plots near scattered villages.

Much of the fighting in the early days raged in swamp forests, sometimes described as damp flats. The swamp forests consisted of scattered trees growing as high as a hundred feet from a plane that remained flooded throughout the rainy season—if not the entire year. Tangled roots braced the towering trees but could not anchor them against gale-force winds when vines and undergrowth reduced visibility on the flooded surfaces to only a few yards.

The vegetation in the mangrove forest was no less formidable. Gigantic trees grew from brackish water deposited at high tide. The mangrove trees varied in height from thirty to sixty feet. They had a visible tangle of thick roots as high as ten feet up the trunk holding the tree solidly in place. Underneath the mangrove canopy, a maze of roots wandered through streams and standing water and impeded movement —this limited visibility to less than fifteen yards.

Both the swamp and mangrove forest grew at sea level. Another form of vegetation was the tropical rain forests that flourished at higher altitudes. Different trees formed an impenetrable double canopy overhead. The surface generally remained open except for low growing ferns or an occasional thicket of vines. Marines walking beneath the canopy could see a standing man as far as fifty yards away. A prone rifleman could remain invisible at a distance of only ten yards.

RAIN AND BITING INSECTS

MONSOON WINDS DROVE rain that drenched the entire island and everyone on it. At the front, heavy rains flooded foxholes.

Conditions weren't much better toward the rear where men slept in jungle hammocks slung between two trees. A Marine would enter his hammock through an opening in a mosquito net and lay down on a rubberized cloth, zipping the net shut. Above him, enclosed in the netting, stretched a rubberized cover designed to shelter him from the rain. Fierce gales like the one that ripped through on the night of D-Day would set the cover flapping like a loose sail and drive the rain inside the hammock.

In the darkness, gusts of winds could uproot trees, weakened by flooding or bombardment, and send them crashing down. A falling tree toppling onto a hammock occupied by one of the Marines could drown him if someone did not slash the covering with a knife.

The rain was like a waterfall pouring down. The first storm lasted five days, and the next storms lasted for weeks. Wet uniforms never dried. Marines continually suffered from fungus infections and jungle rot, which developed into open sores. Mosquito-borne malaria also threatened the Marines' health. They had to contend with aggressive insects: Little red ants, little black ants, and giant red ants on an island where even the caterpillars bite. The Japanese may have endured even more because of medicine shortages and difficulty in distribution, but this was a minor consolation to the Marines beset by disease and discomfort. By the end of January 1944, non-battle injuries or illness had forced over 1,000 Marines to evacuate.

The island's jungles and swamps would have been an ordeal enough without the added rain, wind, and disease. At times, the tormented Marine could see only a few feet in front of him. Movement was nearly impossible, especially with rains flooding the land and turning the volcanic soil into slippery mud. Gen. Shepherd compared the New Britain Campaign to "Grant's fight through the Wilderness in the Civil War."

* * *

Building a relationship with my readers is one of the best things about writing. I occasionally send out emails with details on new releases and special offers. If you'd like to join my free readers group and never miss a new release, go to danielwrinn.com to sign up for the list.

REFERENCES

The information I gathered for Operation Backhander came from several sources. The USMC archives maintained by the Washington National Records Group in Suitland, Maryland, were a source of reference information as well as websites, newspaper articles, and even History Channel documentaries.

First-hand accounts, as recorded by the surviving participants, also contributed to my research. I've cited the main reference books used below:

Coral and Blood: The U.S. Marine Corps' Pacific Campaign, Hammel, Eric (Pacifica, California: Pacifica Military History, 2010.)

The Campaign on New Britain, Hough, Frank O.; Crown, John A. (USMC Historical Monograph. Washington, DC: Historical Division, Division of Public Information, Headquarters U.S. Marine Corps. 1952)

Cartwheel: The Reduction of Rabaul. United States Army in World War II, Miller, John, Jr. (The War in the Pacific. Office of the Chief of Military History, U.S. Department of the Army.1959)

History of United States Naval Operations in World War II, Vol. VII —Aleutians, Gilberts and Marshalls, June 1942–April 1944, Samuel Eliot Morison, (Boston, MA: Little, Brown and Company, 1951.)

ALSO BY DANIEL WRINN

WORLD WAR ONE: WWI HISTORY TOLD FROM THE
TRENCHES, SEAS, SKIES, AND DESERT OF A WAR TORN
WORLD

"Compelling . . . the kind of book that brings history alive." –
Reviewer

**Dive into the incredible history of WWI with
these gripping stories.**

With a unique and fascinating glimpse into the lesser-
known stories of the War to End All Wars, this riveting book
unveils four thrilling stories from the trenches, seas, skies, and
desert of a war-torn world. From one captain's death-defying
mission to smuggle weapons for an Irish rebellion to heroic
pilots and soldiers from all corners of the globe, these stories
shed light on real people and events from one of the greatest
conflicts in human history.

- **WWI: Tales from the Trenches**, a sweeping and eerily realistic narrative which explores the struggles and endless dangers faced by soldiers in the trenches during the heart of WWI
- **Broken Wings**, a powerful and heroic story about one pilot after he was shot down and spent 72 harrowing days on the run deep behind enemy lines
- **Mission to Ireland**, which explores the devious and cunning plan to smuggle a ship loaded with weapons to incite an Irish rebellion against the British
- And **Journey into Eden**, a fascinating glimpse into the lesser-known battles on the harsh and unforgiving Mesopotamian Front

World War I reduced Europe's mightiest empires to rubble, killed twenty million people, and cracked the foundations of our modern world. In its wake, empires toppled, monarchies fell, and whole populations lost their national identities.

Each of these stories brings together unbelievable real-life WWI history, making them perfect for casual readers and history buffs alike. If you want to peer into the past and unearth the incredible stories of the brave soldiers who risked everything, then this book is for you.

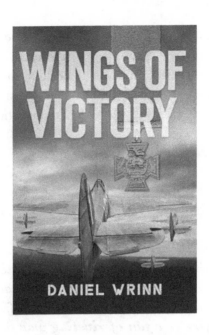

Wings of Victory: World War II adventures in a war-torn Europe

"Historical fiction with a realistic twist." – Reviewer

Thrilling World War II adventures like you've never seen them before.

As the Nazis invade Europe on a campaign for total domination, a brutal war begins to unfold which will change the course of the world forever—and John Archer finds himself caught in the middle of it. When this amateur pilot joins the Allied war effort and is tasked with a series of death-defying missions which place him deep into German-occupied territory, his hair-raising adventures will help decide the fate of Europe.

In **War Heroes**, John is caught up in the devastating Nazi invasion of France while on vacation. Teaming up with ambulance driver Barney, John will need his amateur pilot skills and more than a stroke of luck to pull off the escape of the century.

In **Bombs Over Britain**, the Nazis have a plan which could change the course of the entire war . . . unless Archer can stop them. Air-dropped into Belgium on a top-secret mission, Archer must retrieve vital intelligence and make it out alive. But that's easier said than done when the Gestapo are closing in.

And in **Desert Scout**, Archer finds himself stranded beneath the scorching Libyan sun and in a race against time to turn the tide of the war in North Africa. But with the Luftwaffe and the desert vying to finish him off, can he make it out alive?

Packed with action and filled to the brim with suspense, these thrilling stories combine classic adventures with a riveting and historical World War II setting, making it ideal for history buffs and casual readers. If you're a fan of riveting war fiction novels, WW2 aircraft, and the war for the skies, Archer's next adventure will keep you on the edge of your seat.

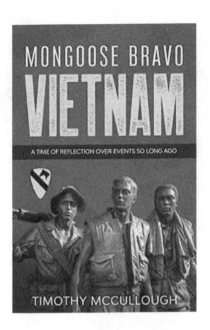

MONGOOSE BRAVO: VIETNAM: A TIME OF REFLECTION OVER
EVENTS SO LONG AGO

"A frank, real, memoir" – Reviewer

**Uncover the gritty, real-life story of a Vietnam
combat veteran.**

With an engaging and authentic retelling of his experi-
ences as an infantry soldier of the B Co., 1/5th 1st Cavalry
Division in the Vietnam War, this gripping account details the
life and struggles of war in a strange and foreign country.

What started as a way of bringing closure to a grieving
mother morphed into a memoir, covering the author's deployment, duty, and eventual return to the United States after the
end of the war. Imbued with the emotion that he felt during
this conflicted time, along with letters and journal entries from
decades ago, this memoir is a testament to the sacrifice that
these brave men and women made fighting on foreign soil.

Recounting the tragedies of war and the chaos of combat
as an infantry soldier, in the words of the author: "We lived,

and fought as a unit, covering each other's backs. Most came home to tell their own stories, many didn't."

If you like gripping, authentic accounts of life and combat during the Vietnam War, then you won't want to miss Mongoose Bravo: Vietnam: A Time of Reflection Over Events So Long Ago.

ABOUT THE AUTHOR

Daniel Wrinn writes Military History & Action Adventure. A US Navy veteran and avid history buff, Daniel lives in the Utah Wasatch Mountains. He writes every day with a view of the snow capped peaks of Park City to keep him company. You can join his readers group and  get notified of new releases, special offers, and free books here:

www.danielwrinn.com